If you were me and lived in...

THE
MAYAN EMPIRE

Carole P. Roman
Illustrated by Paula Tabor

For Michael, Sharon, Eric, and Jennifer

Special thanks to my daughter-in-law, Jennifer, who keeps me on my toes.

Book Design by Kelsea Wierenga

Copyright © 2017 Carole P. Roman

All rights reserved.

ISBN: 153504621X

ISBN 13: 978-1535046213

CreateSpace Independent Publishing Platform, North Charleston, SC

If you were me and lived in...

THE
MAYAN EMPIRE

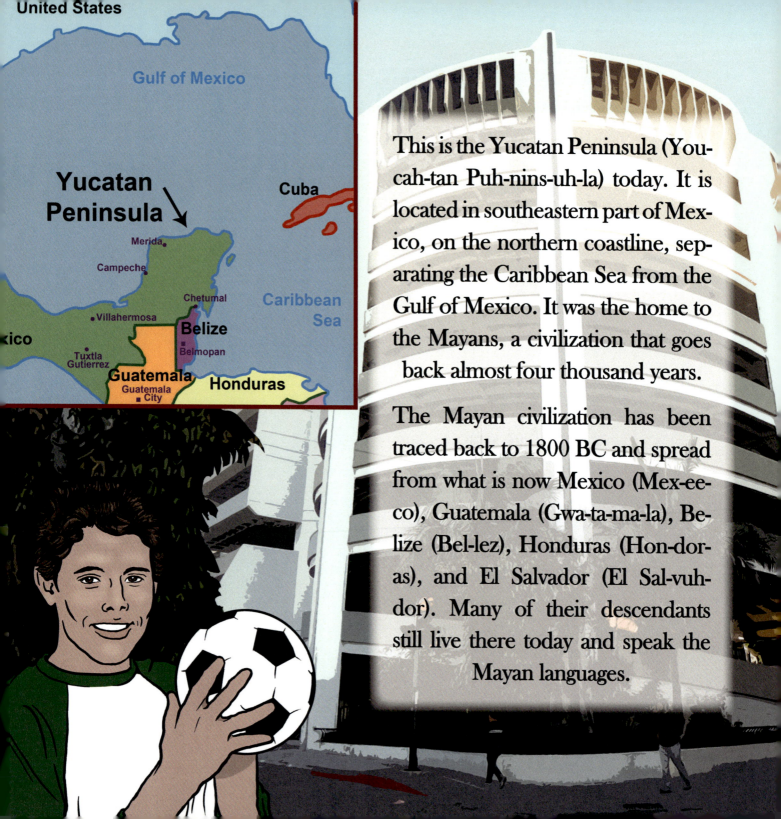

This is the Yucatan Peninsula (You-cah-tan Puh-nins-uh-la) today. It is located in southeastern part of Mexico, on the northern coastline, separating the Caribbean Sea from the Gulf of Mexico. It was the home to the Mayans, a civilization that goes back almost four thousand years.

The Mayan civilization has been traced back to 1800 BC and spread from what is now Mexico (Mex-ee-co), Guatemala (Gwa-ta-ma-la), Belize (Bel-lez), Honduras (Hon-dor-as), and El Salvador (El Sal-vuh-dor). Many of their descendants still live there today and speak the Mayan languages.

This is what a Mayan town might have looked like centuries ago.

If you were me and lived during the Mayan (My-an) civilization, you would be born around 1500 years ago in the year 572 and would have made your home in one of the many Mayan cities.

The Mayans were the only ancient American society with a written account of their history. They recorded their accomplishments on stone billboards called stelas (ste-las), pottery, papers, skins, and anywhere they could report their culture.

The Mayans were indigenous (in-dij-uh-nuhs) people who lived up and down the Yucatan Peninsula.

The whole area was dotted with wealthy city-states that were great areas of activity. The many cities were not unified under one leader. Each town had a king that ruled the land from his palace, located in the center of the metropolis (me-trop-o-lis).

Cities grew along the network of trade routes or a highway. This road was called sacbeob (sak-be-ob), making travel between towns convenient and easy.

People grew rich from the products that made their way up and down the land. Each city had a temple for worship that attracted people to settle, creating centers of exchange and learning.

Your parents chose names carefully for you. If they wanted to name your sister after the moon goddess, they called her Ix Chell (Esh Chel). Ix Kaknab (Esh Ka-nab) meant a woman of the sea. Ikal (I-kal) meant spirit and would be given to a boy like you. Kabil (Ka-bil) was a name that meant good farmer. You were happier to be called spirit rather than a good farmer, especially because you didn't want to work on a farm.

You dreamed of being a scribe for the king. No matter how much you wanted to change your future, you couldn't.

Employment was hereditary in this culture, and people could not change their jobs to improve their lives. If your parents were farmers, then you were destined to be a farmer.

Since your father was a potter, your parents said you had no choice but work in the pottery shed, making pots and dishes. What do the names of the children tell you about what was important to the Mayans?

You might have made your home in the outskirts of the bustling city-state of Tikal (Tik-khal).

Sixty to seventy thousand people lived in the busy area. It was famous for its six large pyramids. You lived there during the Classic Age, and it is remembered as being the Golden Age of Mayan life.

Tikal is an impressive city that rose out of the rainforest like a giant mountain range. The ceremonial and government buildings were placed in the center. There were plazas, ball courts, and markets. The city sprawled to where the residential areas spread on the outskirts.

The city was filled with carved monuments celebrating the deeds of the ruling kings, and you found your home in the shadow of a great wall, separating it from a sacred pyramid.

Your home was built on top of a stone platform, raising it above the rivers of water that flooded the city during the rainy season. After all, the name Tikal means a muddy area, so it is known for being marshy when the weather is wet.

You lived in a simple rectangular home made of clay called adobe (a-doe-bee) with a roof made from hay.

You didn't have nails in Mayan culture, so your house was molded from mud.

Your home was flanked by your grandparents' house on one side and your two uncles' on the other side, creating a compound. The Mayans always lived near their extended family, which included grandparents, aunts, uncles, and cousins. Each member of the family worked to help to create goods for the market or as a gift to the king.

You lived near your mother's family, but soon you were expected to move closer to your father's family, so your father would inherit the family land.

For a while, your father had to work for his in-laws until he could pay the family for marrying your mother. Once he did that, he was able to go back to making pottery. Your mother was happy to stay because parents of Mayan men were known to treat their daughter-in-laws badly. What does this tell you about a women's position in Mayan society?

Eventually, your family would have to move. Mayan women could not inherit any land, and if there were no boys in the family, they would be landless when the parents died.

The wooden floor of your home was raised, and everybody shared a spacious single room. There weren't any windows, and the door always faced east.

It was your job to paint the bottom walls of the house white to brighten up the dark interior. You had to crush seashells, burn them, and add water to make lime to be used as the paint.

Three large stones made up a hearth in the center of the hut for warmth and cooking.

Your mother tended a communal kitchen garden with your aunts. The family ate outdoors under an overhang of thatch in the cooler air on a patio. Men ate first, served by the woman.

You slept on a bed made from branches with a mat placed on top with a cotton blanket.

Life involved hard labor. You lived simply but always had enough to eat. Your mother and sisters worked daily in the garden, cooking, grinding the corn, checking the beehives for honey, and weaving cloth for clothing.

You went with your father to hunt for meat like turkey, dog, turtle, deer, iguana (ig-uan-na), and agouti (ayu-ti), which was a small rodent, as well as fish for the table. You learned to trap wild pigs called peccary (pek-uh-ree).

You had no metal knives to cut the food up and used stones called obsidian (ob-sid-ee-uhn) and flint as sharp-edged tools. Nothing was wasted. Your mother used many of the items from her garden for medicines and dyes for coloring clothes.

You were also responsible for tending the field called milpas (mil-pas) where the maize or corn grew next to squash and beans, your daily diet. You had small crops of tomatoes, papaya (pa-pai-ya), onion, garlic, sweet potatoes, and chili peppers. Your father and you did all the plowing since there were no animals to pull the plow.

You rose early and said a prayer at the shrine in your home. You began by taking care of the daily chores for survival, spending the rest of the day laboring with clay and making useful pottery to sell in the market. After you had sold your work, you had to give the king his share of your profit. The rest belonged to your family. You went home, and after dinner, the family went to sleep when it turned dark outside.

You ate corn at every meal. Maize was the most important food on the table. In the morning, your mother made a dish of porridge called saka (sa-ka) made from maize and chillis. You accompanied your breakfast with a hot, thick drink made from corn called atole (a-tol-eh). At lunchtime, she prepared dumplings of maize dough with a mixture of meat and vegetables inside them. They were wrapped in maize leaves and called tamales (ta-ma-les). For dinner, maize pancakes called tortillas (tor-tee-uhs) were eaten with a stew of meat and vegetables.

You dressed simply, wearing material wrapped around your waist called a loin cloth, but you had a warm poncho (pon-cho) or cape in case it was cold. Your father had a huge turban for his head. Your mother and sisters wore loose blouses and long skirts wrapped around them called a huipil (we-peel).

The women loved to drape themselves in layers of colorful clothes, dressing for comfort rather than show. Sometimes they added a woven sash or belt, and your mother loved a hip wrap, which was a long scarf wound around her hips and tied at the side. In the winter, they used shawls and warm cloaks. Sandals were made out of animal hide and highly decorated.

You carried a woven bag to hold your tools.

Your mother and sisters spent long hours decorating the clothing with bright embroidery. You didn't have much, so you took good care of it to make it last. If there was a festival, you might wear your best clothes, but you made sure to put your good clothes carefully away when you were done wearing them. Clothes were important as they informed others of your position in the community. It served as a type of communication, telling everybody who you were and your place in society.

Your family loved to wear jewelry. Earrings, nose rings, lip rings, pins, and necklaces were made from bits of bone, turtle shell, sea shells, and polished rocks you found.

Wealthy Mayans wore gold, silver, and copper, as well as tall hats. Some wore hats that doubled their height. Only nobles could wear the colorful feathers. If a commoner wore them, he could be killed.

Hair was always worn tied up and well groomed.

You mother crushed the cochineal (co-chi-neal) insects to create a red color to paint her cheeks.

It was a well-known fact that the most attractive Mayans had flat heads and crossed eyes, and your parents made sure you fit in with everyone else's concept of beauty from the day you were born. They worshiped Yum Kaax (Yum Kaahx), the maize god. To honor him, they wanted everything to the look like an ear of corn. An ear of corn has a shape that narrows at the top. The Mayans repeated the design, making an elongated head beautiful.

Your parents bound your head with two boards when you were a newborn, reshaping your skull so that it looked long and your forehead sloped backward. Each day, they made it a bit tighter, so the soft bones would mold to the desired shape. They also tied beads in your hair to hang over the center of your forehead to hit your nose, causing your eyes to cross. They appreciated large noses and created artificial ones that hooked onto the bridge of your nose, reshaping that part of your face as well.

Both your mother and father had colorful tattoos (ta-toos) made with cuts and slashes to their skin rather than needles. It was a sign of courage and bravery that they endured the pain to get them.

Soon, you were planning to file your teeth into sharp points. Rich Mayans decorated their teeth with gemstones.

You were not noble; you came from a family of craftsmen and merchants, making you a commoner or peasant. You loved to look at the grand stone houses the wealthy people owned closer to the king's extravagant palace near the center of the city. The Mayans did not have a middle class, so merchants and craftsmen like your family were either nobles or peasants who created art or owned businesses. Craftsmen who had peasants' existences were a step up from the lives of farmers, but they could not act or dress like a noble. They were born peasants, and if they forgot that, they risked death.

You understood that, sadly, you could never be anything but a pottery maker like your father.

You knew that commoners were divided into prosperous ones like merchants, such as skilled craftsmen like your father, or poor laborers who farmed or fished. Mayan society had five main levels with the king at the top of society. The king's power was hereditary, which meant that his oldest son would become king when he died. The nobility, which was made of the well-connected class or almehenob' (al-meh-nob), came next. They were the wealthiest and closest to the king. The leading generals could be found in this group of people.

Next was the priesthood, called ah'kinob' (ah-kin-ob). They were more powerful than others since they lead all the religious ceremonies. They spoke directly to the gods and controlled the sacrifices. It was believed that the gods would tell the priests what the farmers should plant or harvest. They also decided if people went to war. Whatever social class in which your family belonged, the gods' decisions were final. Religion was an important part of Mayan life, and the priests had the final say in everything people did. They could determine who lived or died.

Another level of people were the commoners, ah'chembal uinieol' (ah-chem-bal uin-ie-ol) or your group. Most people were in this category and were farmers. Lastly came the slaves or pencat'ob' (pen-cat-ob). Slaves were caught during wars. The Mayans did not use their people as slaves. Slaves were captured from other tribes.

Although women didn't have much power, sometimes when a king was under-aged, they could help him rule. There were also female priestesses in certain sacred places, and women played a role in the marketplace selling products. Your mother took care of the family shrine to the gods.

Mayans did not have coins for currency. They had large markets where people met and traded for what they needed. They sold their surplus crops in exchange for cloth or tools. Instead of coins, they traded cacao (ca-ca-o) beans, gold, copper bells, jade, and oyster shell beads as forms of money.

There was no formal school for the children of your class. Your job was to learn from and help your parents. When you turned four-years-old, you were given daily jobs, like getting clay from the riverbed to help your father make his pots.

By the time you turned fifteen, you would be considered a grown-up. You would move to a house of your own nearby the compound and live as an adult. Your parents were already looking for a wife for you! Your sister followed your mother all day, tending the garden, cooking, cleaning, and working the loom to make clothing for the family.

In the ancient Mayan society, the priest's job was to teach only the children of nobles. They taught math, science, medicine, astronomy, writing, and engineering. Mayans were capable of building complex cities and beautiful temples that many said coordinated their placement with the constellations in the sky. They were able to predict solar eclipses, had an accurate calendar, and used astrological cycles to forecast both the planting and harvesting of the crops. This knowledge was held by a few people in the population, and that was the way they wanted to keep it.

The Mayan written language was made up of eight-hundred symbols. Each symbol represented a part of a word or a whole word and could be combined into countless combinations. Learning to read and write would involve many hours, more hours than a boy who worked in a potter's shed could spare.

Life wasn't all about work. Every twenty days, there was a religious festival, and everybody would go to the city to sing and dance as they joined the celebrations.

You were able to see the priest communicate with the many gods! The priests danced in scary costumes on the steps of the temples. After a while, other dancers joined them. They also wore feathered costumes with huge headdresses.

There were delicious feasts, and you might catch a game of Pok-ta-Tok (Pok-ta-Tok) which was a fast-paced ball game.

Players threw a five-pound rubber ball. Using only their forearms and thighs, they had to pass and hit the ball into hoops on either side of the court. Each team member wore a distinctive headdress to show which team he belonged.

The special day of your coming of age ceremony was arriving soon. On your fifteenth birthday, you would be considered an adult.

Your parents would make you a fine feast with lots of guests to help you celebrate. They would arrange a marriage with a suitable girl, and your life as a grown-up would begin.

You believed and worshiped many different gods.

All gods had a good and bad side to them. The most important god was Izamna (Et-sam-nah), who was known as the creator as well as the fire and earth god. Kukulan (Ku-kol-kan) was frequently pictured in works of art and an important god. He was depicted as a feathered serpent. Chac (Chaac) was the god of rain and lighting. Only a priest or a king could talk directly to the gods.

So you see, if you were me, how life in the Mayan Empire could really be.

Mayan Contributions to the World

The Mayans created a calendar more accurate than the ones used in Europe. In the field of medicine, they performed surgical operations on the brain.

The Mayans were incredible mathematicians. Their numerical system was similar to that of the Romans, but instead of X's and I's they use dots, bars, and shells. Each dot had the value of one, each bar the value of five, and each shell the value of zero.

The most important mathematical contribution of the Mayans is the concept of zero. The Mayans were the first to develop the number that isn't really a number of anything. Imagine finding a word to mean something that never existed and has no value.

The Mayans mapped the night skies without the aid of a telescope!

Using their knowledge of the skies and stars, they understood that a solar year was slightly more than 365 days. This calendar was divided into eighteen months consisting of twenty days. They also added five unlucky days at the end of their calendar, a reason only understood by them.

The Mayans also had an intricate system known as the long count calendar, which ultimately measures a period of over five-thousand years.

Despite these accomplishments of the Mayans, they never discovered the use of the wheel.

Many foods like chocolate, corn, turkeys, squash, tropical fruits, were introduced by the Mayans. They farmed and used cotton widely. Mayan weaving is highly sought after and their textiles are considered some of the best examples in the world.

Famous Names in Mayan Culture

Itzamn (Et-sam-nah)- a great Mayan warrior and leader of the Mayan people. He was considered to be the sun god. Legends say he came from across the sea and magically parted the waters so the people could come into the land.

Kukulcan (Ko-kol-kan)- an important priest and the founder of the Mayan kingdom. He divided the Mayans into four manageable tribes, then appointed a royal family to rule each faction.

Muwaan Mat (Mwah-n Mat)- the queen of the Mayan city, Palenque, and ruled from 612 through 615 AD. She was otherwise known as Lady Beastie.

Lady Yohl Ik'nal (Johl-Ik-nal) of Palenque (Pa-leng-kay)- Muwaan Mat's mother, as well as the Mayan city-state, Palenque's queen from 583 AD and ruled until her death in the year 604 AD.

Lady Eveningstar of Yaxchilan (Ev-en-ing-star of Yahs-chee-laun)- the wife and queen consort of the reigning Mayan king of Yaxchilan.

Lady of Tikal (Tik-khal)- named Woman of Tikal, she was the queen of Tikal, a Mayan city. She was queen from 511 to 527 AD.

Lady Six Sky of Naranjo (Six Sky Nar-an-ho)- the queen of the Mayan city of Naranjo from 682 to 741 AD. Her ruling was the most remarkable because she established a new dynasty. She instructed monuments to be made observing the important rituals she would perform and was depicted in these monuments as a warrior-leader standing over prisoners, which was a rare portrayal of a woman for those times.

Lady K'abel (Kah-a-bel)- her tomb was discovered recently, and she was the military ruler between AD 672 and 692. One of the artworks found in the tomb describes her as Lady Snake Lord, revealing the Lady K'able was a member of the powerful Snake dynasty of Calakmul (Kah-lak-mool).

Glossary

adobe (a-doe-bee)- a brick or building material of sun-dried earth and straw.

Almehenob' (Al-meh-nob)- a social class also known as kings, consisted of the local town authorities such as lords, policemen, and town council members.

ah'kinob' (ah-kin-ob)- meaning they of the sun or they of time. This title was given to a group of high-ranking priests. Their responsibility was to share with people the connections between the worship of gods and actions such as arrivals, departures, and partnerships.

ah'chembal uinieol' (ah-chem-bal uin-ie-ol)- the common people.

agouti (ayu-ti)- a large rodent that is used for meat by Mayan people.

astronomy (as-tron-o-mee)- the study of the sky and all the objects in it.

ātōlli (a-tol-eh)- a traditional hot corn drink.

Belize (Be-lez)- a country in Central America, on the eastern coast of Central America.

Caribbean (ka-rih-bee-an)- the Caribbean is home to many islands and runs along Central and South American coasts filled with people enriched in the caribbean culture.

cochineal (co-chi-neal)- a red dye consisting of the dried bodies of female cochineal insects.

commoner (com-mon-er)- an ordinary person without rank or title.

compound (com-pound)- to form by combining parts.

constellations (con-stel-lay-shuns)- groups of stars that form recognizable patterns.

craftsman (krafts-man)- a skilled worker at a craft.

eclipse (eh-clips)- the obstruction of the moon's light being blocked by another object.

El Salvador (El Sal-vuh-dor)- a country in northwest Central America.

embroidery (em-broy-der-ree)- decorating clothing with small designs made with needle and thread.

exotic (ig-zadik)- a unique item or animal from a foreign country.

Guatemala (Gwa-te-ma-la)- a country in Central America that gained its independence from Spain in 1821.

hearth (harth)- the floor in front of or inside a fireplace.

hereditary (he-red-i-ta-ree)- having title or possession through inheritance or because of birth.

Honduras (Hon-dor-as)- a country in northern Central America.

huipil (we-peel)- a traditional shirt worn by women in Mexico and Central America. The shirt is usually in a rectangle-like shaped cotton and embroidered to represent the women's locale.

Ikal (I-kal)- a popular boy's name.

iguana (ig-uan-na)- a large greenish lizard.

indigenous (in-dij-uh-nuhs)- produced, living, or existing naturally in a particular region or environment.

Ix Chell (Esh Chel)- a popular girl's name. Ix Chell is a Mayan goddess of the moon, water, weaving, and childbirth.

Ix Kaknab (Esh Kak-nab)- means women of the sea.

Kabil (Ka-bil)- means good farmer and can be used as a boy's name.

lime (lim)- a dry white powder consisting essentially of calcium hydroxide that is made by treating quicklime with water.

loincloth (loin-cloth)- a cloth worn about the hips often as the sole article of clothing in warm climates.

loom (loom)- a machine for interweaving two or more sets of threads or yarns to form a cloth.

maize (mei-z)- a tall widely cultivated American cereal grass (Zea mays), bearing seeds on elongated ears.

Mayans (My-ans)- the Mayan civilization came from the Mesoamerican civilization. They are well-known for their fully formed writings as well as their art, architecture, mathematics, calendar, and astronomical systems.

metropolis (me-trop-o-lis)- a large or important city.

Mexico (Mex-ee-co)- the country located in the southern part of North America.

milpas- a small field in Mexico or Central America that is cleared from trees, then used for farming for a few seasons, and abandoned for a new clearing.

noble (no-bel)- belonging to the highest social class: of, relating to, or belonging to the nobility.

obsidian (uh-b-sid-ee-uhn)- a dark natural glass that forms when lava cools.

patio (pat-ee-o)- an outdoor space next to a home used for eating or recreation.

papaya (pa-pai-ya)- a sweet tropical fruit.

peccary (pek-uh-ree)- largely nocturnal gregarious American mammals resembling pigs.

peccary (pek-uh-ree)- largely nocturnal gregarious American mammals resembling pigs.

pencat'ob' (pen-cat-ob)- the lowest class of the Mayan class structure, known as slaves.

plaza (pla-za)- a great courtyard in a central location in a city, used for events like parades and religious ceremonies.

poncho (pon-cho)- a blanket with a slit in the middle so that it can be slipped over the head and worn as a sleeveless garment.

porridge (pawr-idge)- a soft food made by boiling meal of grains or legumes in milk or water until thick.

priests (pree-st-s)- a male in the Mayan religion given the right to perform ceremonies and act as a representative between humans and gods.

priestesses- females in the Mayan religion given the right to perform ceremonies and act as a representative between humans and gods.

profit (pro-fit)- the money left over after all the expenses are eliminated.

pyramid (pir-a-mid)- a large triangular building.

sacbeob (sak-be-ob)- a word used to describe the continuous architectural appearances connecting the Mayan communities.

saka (sa-ka)- any of the numerous nomadic peoples who used to live in the steeplands.

sacred (say-cred)- highly valued and important, deserving great respect.

sacrifice (sac-ra-fice)- an act of killing a person or animal in a religious ceremony as an offering to please a god.

...e (shrin)- a place that is considered holy and where people go to pray.

...tatus (sta-us)- a person's place in the community.

stelas (ste-las)- sculptures and monuments that the Mayans sculpted out of stone shafts during the Classic period.

tamale (ta-ma-le)- a Mexican food that's made up of seasoned ground meat or beans rolled in cornmeal, wrapped in a corn husk, and steamed.

tattoos (tat-toos)- the art of cutting or imprinting designs on the human body.

thatch (tha-ch)- to make (a roof) with dried plant material.

Tikal (Tik-khal)- the Mayan ruins of a natural preserve founded in the Guatemalan rainforest.

tortillas (tor-tee-uhs)- round, thin Mexican bread that is usually eaten hot with a filling of meat, cheese, etc.

turban (tur-bun)- a head covering that is worn by men in some parts of the world that is made of a long cloth wrapped around the head.

Yucatan Peninsula (You-cah-tan Puh-nins-uh-la)- a piece of land in southeastern Mexico that is largely surrounded by water and splits in between the Gulf of Mexico from the Caribbean Sea.

Yum Kaax (Yum Kaahx)- means lord of the forest, named by the Mayans for the god of natural vegetation and guardian of animals.

Made in the USA
Middletown, DE
02 August 2017